j 743.6 Bal

W9-CFB-785

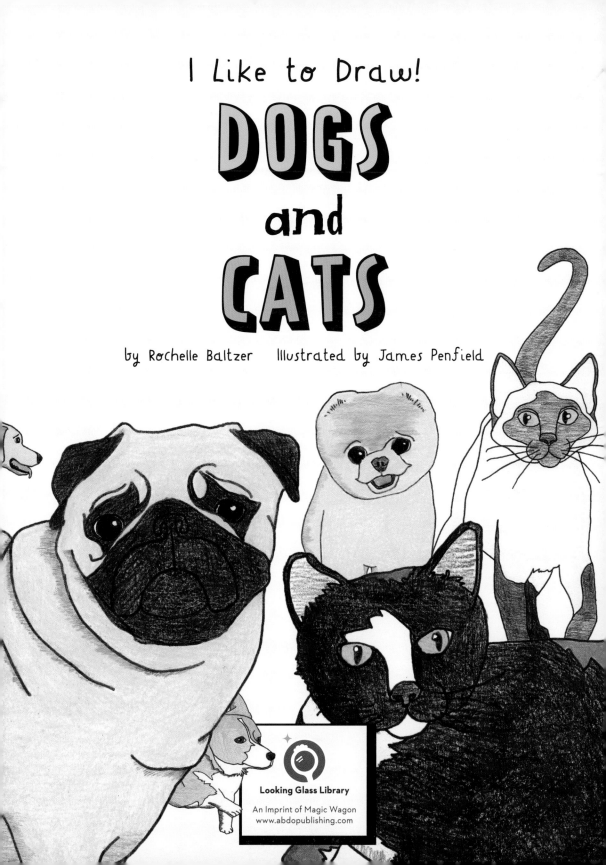

I Like to Draw!

DOGS
and
CATS

by Rochelle Baltzer   Illustrated by James Penfield

Looking Glass Library

An Imprint of Magic Wagon
www.abdopublishing.com

www.abdopublishing.com

Published by Magic Wagon, a division of ABDO, PO Box 398166, Minneapolis, Minnesota 55439. Copyright © 2015 by Abdo Consulting Group, Inc. International copyrights reserved in all countries. No part of this book may be reproduced in any form without written permission from the publisher. Looking Glass library™ is a trademark and logo of Magic Wagon.

Printed in the United States of America, North Mankato, Minnesota.
102014
012015

Cover and Interior Elements and Photos: iStockphoto, Thinkstock

Written by Rochelle Baltzer
Illustrations by James Penfield
Edited by Heidi M. D. Elston, Megan M. Gunderson, Bridget O'Brien
Cover and interior design by Candice Keimig

Library of Congress Cataloging-in-Publication Data

Baltzer, Rochelle, 1982- author.
   Dogs and cats / Written by Rochelle Baltzer ; Illustrated by James Penfield.
      pages cm. -- (I Like to Draw!)
   Includes index.
   ISBN 978-1-62402-082-7
1. Dogs in art--Juvenile literature. 2. Cats in art--Juvenile literature. 3. Drawing--Technique--Juvenile literature. I. Penfield, James, illustrator. II. Title.
   NC783.8.D64B35 2015
   743.6'97--dc23
                          2014031851

MEOW MEOW

Cats Rule!
Dogs drool!

Purr Purr!
Purr Purr!
Purr Purr!

TABLE of CONTENTS

DOGS and CATS

Dogs and cats have been our companions for thousands of years. From rescue work to herding sheep, dogs have performed valuable roles in society. Cats have filled other roles, such as hunting rodents. Perhaps most important, dogs and cats are treasured pets around the world. Let's learn how to draw your favorite dogs and cats!

STUFF YOU'LL NEED

Pencil

Paper

Eraser

Marker

Colored Pencils

KNOW THE BASICS

SHAPES

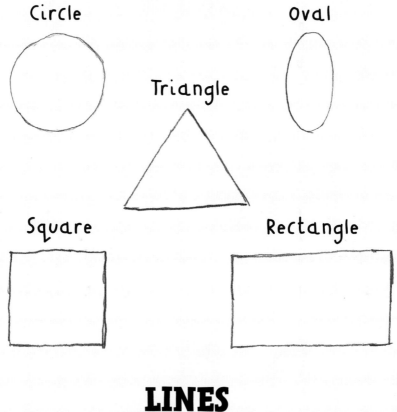

Circle

Oval

Triangle

Square

Rectangle

LINES
thick & thin

Straight

Wavy

Jagged

TALK LIKE AN ARTIST

Composition

Composition is the way parts of a drawing or picture are arranged. Balanced composition means having an even amount of parts, such as lines and shapes.

Unbalanced

Balanced

Dimension

Dimension is the amount of space an object takes up. Drawings are created on a flat surface and have length and width but not depth. So, they are two-dimensional. You can give an object depth by layering colors and adding shadow. This makes it look like it's popping off the page!

Without Dimension

With Dimension

Shadow

Shadow is created by the way light shines on an object. Look outside on a sunny day. See how the sunlight shines on a tree? The side of the tree with more sunlight appears lighter than the other side.

Without Shadow

With Shadow

PUG

The pug is often called "a lot of dog in a little body." Its strong personality is part of what makes it so lovable. Pugs are loyal and want to please their owners. They are originally from China and are usually **fawn** or black in color. The pug is known for its wrinkled face, muscular body, and tightly curled tail.

1 Draw a circle for the head, a circle for the snout, and an oval for the body.

2 Add lines for the legs and two rounded triangles for the ears. Don't forget the curly pug tail!

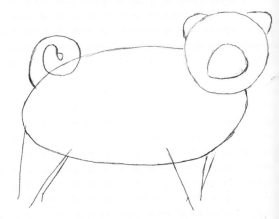

3 Draw details on the head and face. Outline the legs and body.

4 Add final details to the face, body, and feet.

ART TIP
The harder you push on your pencil, the thicker and darker your line will be.

5 Outline the finished drawing with a thin, black marker.

6 Color your pug! This one is fawn.

Snore Fest
A pug's short nose can cause it to snore!

9

POMERANIAN

The perky Pomeranian is a cheerful companion for many people. It is smart and aims to make its owners happy. Pomeranians are bold, playful, and alert. Originally from Pomerania (now Germany), they were bred down from sled and herding dogs. They weigh just three to seven pounds (1 to 3 kg). The Pomeranian is known for its thick double coat and pointed, foxlike face.

1 Draw circles for the head, snout, and body.

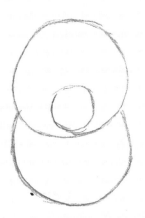

2 Add lines for the legs, and draw rounded ears.

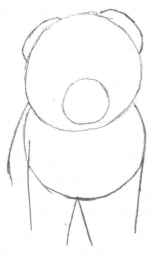

3 Finish outlining the body and feet. Detail the face.

4 Add final detail to the face, body, and feet.

5 Outline the finished drawing with a thin, black marker.

6 Finish this little guy by coloring in light tan fur.

Cute as a Teddy Bear

A Pomeranian named Boo became a popular dog on the Internet. He has a teddy bear haircut, which helps prevent **matting**.

ENGLISH BULLDOG

The English bulldog is one of the most mellow dog breeds. Its gentle yet protective manner makes it a popular dog for families. Bulldogs are **confident** and can be **stubborn**. They originated in Great Britain and have a short coat that often has **blotches** or spots. The bulldog is known for its short, muscular body, noticeable under bite, and slow-moving shuffle.

1 Draw circles for the head and snout.
Draw an oval for the body.

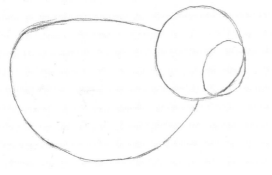

2 Add lines for the legs and a little, stumpy tail.

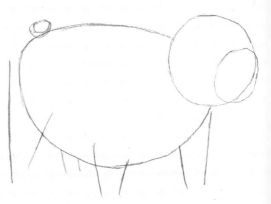

3 Add details to the head and face.
Outline the body, legs, and tail.

4 Bulldogs are husky, so give yours some neck rolls! Then finish detailing the legs, body, and face.

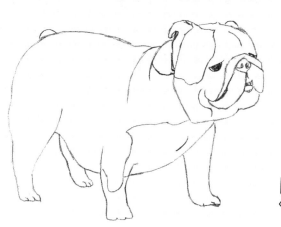

ART TIP
Add spots to the bulldog if you want. Just draw shapes to define areas of color on its face or body.

5 Outline the finished drawing with a thin, black marker.

6 Color your bulldog. This one is solid with blotches.

Excuse Me
The bulldog has a pushed-in nose with small nostrils. It often breathes with its mouth open, gulping air. So, it has a lot of gas!

13

PEMBROKE WELSH CORGI

The corgi is the smallest type of herding dog. Originally from Wales, *corgi* means "dwarf dog" in Welsh. The corgi has a long, low body and a thick coat. The Pembroke Welsh corgi has pointed ears, in contrast to the Cardigan Welsh corgi's rounded ears. Its color can be red, **sable**, black, **fawn**, or tan, and it can have white markings. The corgi is active, agreeable, and **affectionate**.

1 Draw a circle for the head, an oval for the body, and a rounded triangle for the snout.

2 Draw lines for the legs and a half circle for the hip. This corgi is running!

3 Add details to the face and body, and draw triangles for the ears. Finish outlining the legs.

4 Add more details to the corgi's fur, face, and ears. Draw lines on the body to help show dimension.

5 Outline the finished drawing with a thin, black marker.

6 Color your corgi! This one is fawn with white markings.

C'mon, Guys! A corgi may try to herd its owners!

STANDARD POODLE

Unlike what many people think, the poodle is not French. The **breed** began in Germany, assisting hunters in water. Poodles are smart, **obedient**, and social. Many poodles work as Seeing Eye dogs or therapy dogs. The poodle has a thick, curly coat that is white, black, apricot, or gray. The standard poodle has been bred down to two other sizes: miniature and toy.

1 Draw circles for the head and body. Draw a rounded rectangle for the snout.

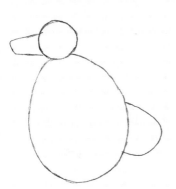

2 Add lines to the body for the legs. Don't forget the tail! Keep in mind the poodle's puffy, shaped coat.

3 Define the legs, face, and body. Add an eye, nose, and mouth.

4 Give the poodle its famous puffy coat! Outline it with a wavy line, defining its curls. Finish detailing the legs and face.

ART TIP
A dog or cat's coat can be drawn by using straight, jagged, or wavy lines, depending on the type!

5 Outline the finished drawing with a thin, black marker.

6 Color your poodle. This one is black. Shade it to add dimension.

Posh with a Purpose
Hunters made up the traditional poodle haircut. This cut helped the dogs stay warm in water.

LABRADOR RETRIEVER

The loyal Labrador retriever is the most popular dog **breed** in the United States. It's easy to see why. Its friendly manner and **affectionate**, playful personality make the Lab a good family dog. Labs were first bred in Newfoundland, Canada, to retrieve fishing nets. They have short, water-resistant coats. Labs come in three colors: yellow, black, and chocolate, or brown.

1 Draw a circle for the head, an oval for the body, and a rounded rectangle for the snout.

2 Draw lines off the body for the legs and tail. This Lab is shown "pointing," or showing its owner that it has spotted something to hunt.

3 Add more detail to the head, legs, and body. Draw in feet, and give the Lab an ear.

4 Detail the feet and face. This Lab is ready to go!

ART TIP
Start with a balanced composition of shapes from the first step. This gives the final drawing a stronger feel.

5 Outline the finished drawing with a thin, black marker.

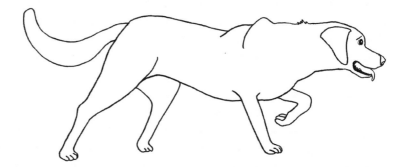

6 Color your Lab. This one is yellow.

Leaping Labs
Labs love to swim and have strong legs for leaping into water. The world record leap for a Lab is 27 feet (8 m)!

PERSIAN CAT

The Persian is a popular cat **breed**. It is known for its long coat. It has the longest coat of any cat breed! People love the Persian's sweet, gentle nature and big, expressive eyes. This cat has a broad, short body and heavy-boned legs. These features make the Persian more likely to lounge around than leap!

1 Draw three circular shapes for the head, body, and tail.

2 Add lines for the legs and two triangles for the ears.

3 Give the Persian its wild fur by drawing jagged lines around the head, body, and tail. Add eyes, a nose, and a mouth.

4 Detail the fur a bit more to show dimension. Define the feet, and give the cat some whiskers!

ART TIP
Be aware of how many whiskers you add. Shoot for balance within the composition.

5 Outline the finished drawing with a thin, black marker.

6 Color your Persian cat. This one is white with green eyes.

Old Favorites
Persian cats are originally from Persia (now Iran) in the 1600s. They are one of the oldest cat **breeds.**

SIAMESE CAT

The Siamese cat was once thought of as **sacred** in Siam (now Thailand). It has almond-shaped blue eyes, dark **points**, and a long, thin body. The Siamese is known to be loud. It is the most **vocal** house cat! The Siamese is smart and likes to play. It also enjoys lying in its owner's lap.

 1 Draw two circles for the head and the snout. Then, add an oval for the body.

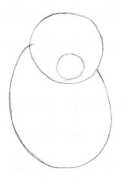

2 Draw lines for the legs, two triangles for the ears, and a curled tail.

 3 Outline the entire body and head. Then add detail to the face, including the eyes, nose, and mouth.

4 Draw lines on the body where you want the cat's points to be. Finish detailing the feet and face. Add whiskers!

ART TIP
The curve of a cat's tail indicates different emotions. Explore this idea by changing the position or shape of the tail!

5 Outline the finished drawing with a thin, black marker.

6 Color this Siamese if you please! This one is white with black points. Don't forget to color the eyes blue!

Points of Interest
Siamese cats are born pure white. The color on their **points** comes in as they get older.

CALICO CAT

The calico is not a **breed** of cat. Calico refers to the cat's coloring. Calico cats are white, with some orange and black patches. Sixteen different cat breeds can have the calico pattern. They include the Persian, Manx, and Scottish fold.

1 Draw a circle for the head, a long oval for the body, and a curved line for the tail.

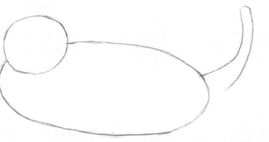

2 Draw lines for the legs and triangles for the ears.

3 Detail the face, including the eyes, nose, and mouth. Define the ears, and add detail to the body and legs.

4 Finish the legs and feet. Add final details to the face, including whiskers. Finally, draw jagged lines where you want the calico's fur markings to be.

ART TIP
Draw simple, curved lines to the body of a cat or dog. This makes it look more realistic because it gives the animal dimension.

5 Outline the finished drawing with a thin, black marker.

6 Color your calico! This one is mostly black with some orange and white. Be creative, and add as much color as you want!

Girly Cats
Because of their **genetics**, calico cats are almost always female.

SPHYNX CAT

The sphynx cat is known for its hairless, wrinkled body and large, pointed ears. It is energetic and doesn't shy away from being the center of attention. The sphynx is a loyal companion and enjoys spending time with its owners. Because it lacks fur, this cat likes to nestle under a blanket to keep warm.

1 Draw two circles for the head and snout. Then, draw a long oval for the body. Add a thin, curved tail.

2 Add lines for the legs and triangles for the ears.

3 Fill in the face with details. Then, outline the legs and add details to the body, including wrinkly skin!

4 Finish the face and ears, and add short whiskers. Curve your wrinkle lines to match the curves of the body.

ART TIP
Not all cats have whiskers. Some sphynx cats do not. Try drawing one without whiskers to see how this changes the look of the final drawing!

5 Outline the finished drawing with a thin, black marker.

6 Add color to your sphynx. All the usual cat markings can be found on sphynx skin. So, add some spots if you want!

Fuzzy Feel
A sphynx can have a thin layer of fuzz on its body, making it feel like a peach!

LOOK WHAT YOU CAN DRAW!

The Truth about CATS and DOGS

Cats can make more than 100 vocal sounds,
but dogs can make only 10.

Most cats do not have eyelashes.

Cats can be trained to use a toilet!

Dogs have twice as many muscles
in their ears as humans.

The smartest dog breeds can
understand about 250 words.

A dog usually has 42 teeth,
while a human typically has 32.

Glossary

affectionate (uh-FEHK-shuh-nuht) – showing feelings of love.

blotch – a large, uneven spot.

breed – a group of animals sharing the same ancestors and appearance.

confident – sure of oneself.

fawn – a light grayish brown color.

genetics – the study of how features are inherited.

matting – forming into a tangled mass.

obedient (oh-BEE-dee-uhnt) – willing to obey commands.

point – body parts of a Siamese cat (face, ears, feet, and tail) that have darker fur.

sable – having black-tipped hairs on a silver, gold, gray, fawn, or brown background.

sacred (SAY-kruhd) – connected with the worship of a god.

stubborn – not wanting to change one's ideas or stop doing something.

vocal – expressing oneself freely or loudly.

Websites

To learn more about I Like to Draw!, visit **booklinks.abdopublishing.com**. These links are routinely monitored and updated to provide the most current information available.

Index